Microservices Architecture Handbook

*Non-Programmer's
Guide for Building
Microservices*

1

You can connect with me at:

Email: valueadd2life@gmail.com

Facebook Page:@sflemingauthor

Respective authors own all copyrights not held by the publisher.

The information herein is offered for informational purposes solely and is universal as so. The presentation of the information is without a contract or any type of guarantee assurance.

The trademarks that are used are without any consent, and the publication of the trademark is without permission or backing by the trademark owner. All trademarks and brands within this book are for clarifying purposes only and are owned by the owners themselves, not affiliated with this document.

BONUS MICROSERVICES BOOKLET

Dear Friend,

I am privileged to have you onboard. You have shown faith in me and I would like to reciprocate it by offering the maximum value with an amazing gift. I have been researching on the topic and have an excellent "Microservices Booklet" for you to take your own expedition on the subject to next level.

- Do you want to know the best online courses to begin exploring the topic?
- Do you want to know major success stories of Microservices implementation?
- What are the latest trends and news?

Also, do you want once in a while updates on interesting implementation of latest Technology; especially those impacting lives of common people? "Get Instant Access to Free Booklet and Future Updates"

Type Link: **http://eepurl.com/ds8sfD**

or

QR Code: You can download a QR code reader app on your mobile and open the link by scanning below:

Contents

1. Introduction

As the disruption of technologies continues to play a role in our lives, the application development process is becoming more flexible and agile. You must have heard about the concepts of Agile, DevOps, Kanban and many more. All these terminologies are basically making the application of development or the program writing exercise more flexible, more independent, and faster.

The Microservices architecture develops an application as a collection of loosely coupled services which is meant for different business requirements. Therefore, this architecture supports the continuous delivery/deployment of large, complex applications. It also enables the organization to evolve its application development capabilities.

Who can use this book?

This book can be used by a beginner, Technology Consultant, Business Consultant and Project Manager who are not into so much coding. The structure of the book is such that it answers the most asked questions about Microservices. It also covers the best and the latest case studies with benefits. Therefore, it is expected that after going through this book, you can discuss the topic with any stakeholder and take your agenda ahead as per your role. Additionally, if you are new to the industry, and looking for an application development job, this book will help you to prepare with all the relevant information and understanding of the topic.

2. Introduction to Monolith and Microservices

In May 2011, a workshop of software architects was held in Venice and coined the term "Microservices" to relate to an upcoming software architectural technique that many of the software architectures had been researching. It wasn't until May 2012 that Microservices was approved to be the most appropriate term to describe a style of software development. The first case study relating to Microservices architecture was presented by James Lewis in March 2012, at the 33rd Degree in Krakow in Microservices-Java the Unix way. To date, numerous presentations about Microservices have been made at various conferences worldwide, with software architects presenting different designs and software components of Microservices and its integration to different platforms and interfaces, such as Microsoft architecture and URI interface. Currently, Microservices has grown incredibly and has become an ideal way of developing small business applications, thanks to its efficiency and scalability. This software development technique is particularly perfect for developing software or applications compatible with a range of devices, both developed and yet to be developed, and platforms.

Microservices Defined

A standard definition of Microservices is not yet available, but it can be described as a technique of software application development which entails developing a single application as a suite of independently deployable, small, modular service. Every service controls processes and communicates with each other through a well-defined, lightweight mechanism, often an HTTP resource API to serve a business goal. Microservices are built around business capabilities and are independently deployable by a fully automated deployment mechanism. They can be written in different programming languages such, as Java and C++ and employ different data storage technologies to be effective in the central management of enterprises or small businesses.

Microservices communicate to one other in several ways based on the requirements of the application employed in its development. Many developers use HTTP/REST with JSON or Protobuf for efficient communication. To choose the most suitable communication protocol, you must be a DevOps professional, and in most situations, REST (Representation State Transfer) communication protocol is preferred due to its lower complexity compared to other protocols.

Monolith Defined

A monolith is a software application whose modules cannot be executed independently.

This makes monoliths are difficult to use in distributed systems without specific frameworks or ad hoc solutions, such as Network Objects, RMI or CORBA. However, even these approaches still endure the general issues that affect monoliths, as discussed below.

Problems of Monoliths

1. Large-size monoliths are hard to maintain and evolve due to their complexity. Finding bugs requires long perusals through their code base.

2. Monoliths also suffer from the "dependency hell," in which adding or updating libraries results in inconsistent systems that either do not compile/run or, worse, misbehave.

3. Any change in one module of a monolith requires rebooting the whole application. For large projects, restarting usually entails considerable downtimes, hindering the development, testing, and maintenance of the project.

4. Deployment of monolithic applications is usually suboptimal due to conflicting requirements on the constituent models' resources: some can be memory-intensive, others computational-intensive and others require ad hoc components (e.g. SQL-based, rather than graph-based databases). When choosing a deployment environment, the developer must compromise with a one-size-fits-all configuration, which is either expensive or suboptimal with respect to the individual modules.

5. Monoliths limit scalability. The usual strategy for handling increments of inbound requests is to create new instances of the same application and to split the load amongst said instances. Moreover, it could be the increased traffic stresses only a subset of the modules, making the allocation of the newer resources for the other components inconvenient.

6. Monoliths also represent a technology lock-in for developers, which are bound to use the same language and frameworks of the original application

7. The Microservices architectural style has been proposed to cope with such problems as discussed above.

Monolithic Architecture   Microservices Architecture

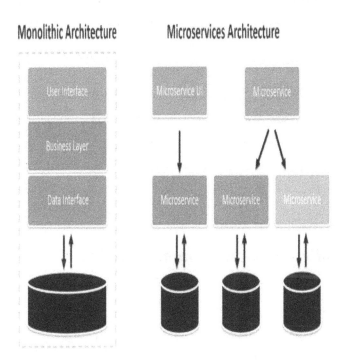

Future of Microservices

Over the years, software application development has evolved from Service-Oriented Architecture (SOA) to monolith architecture and now microservices architecture, which is the most preferred software application technique. Global organizations such as Amazon, eBay, Twitter, PayPal, The Guardian, and many others have not only migrated but also embraced microservices over SOA and Monolith architectures in developing their websites and applications. Will Microservices be the future of software application development? Time will tell.

Microservices compared to SOA

Microservices vs. SOA has generated lots of debate amongst software application developers, with some arguing that microservices is simply a refined improved version of SOA, while others consider microservices as a whole new concept in software application development which does not relate in any way with SOA. Nonetheless, microservices have a lot of similarities to SOA. The main difference between SOA and microservices may be thought to lie in the size and scope as suggested by the term "micro, "meaning small. Therefore, microservices are significantly smaller compared to SOA and are deployed as an independent single unit. Furthermore, an SOA entails either numerous microservices or a single monolith. This debate can be concluded by referring to SOA as a relative of microservices. Nevertheless, they all perform the same role as software programme development, albeit in different ways.

* Refer the below IT spending forecast for FY 2018. It clearly shows the mounting pressure to make the processes more efficient.

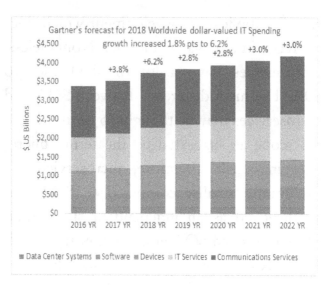

Source: Gartner Market Databook, 4Q17

Features of Microservices Architecture

The features of microservices architecture differ widely as not all microservices have the same properties. However, we have managed to come up with several features that may be deemed appropriate and repetitive in almost all microservices.

Independent Deployment

Microservices are autonomous and can be

deployed separately, making them less likely to cause system failures. This is done using components, which are defined as a unit of software that is independently replaceable and upgradeable. In addition to components, microservices architecture utilizes libraries or services. Libraries are components attached to a program using in-memory function calls. On the other hand, services are out-of-process components that communicate through different mechanisms, such as web service request mechanism Microservices applications. Software componentization involves breaking them into miniature components, termed as services. A better microservices architecture uses services as components rather than libraries since they are independently deployable. An application consisting of multiple libraries cannot be deployed separately in a single process since a single change to any component results in the development and deployment of the entire application. An application consisting of multiple services is flexible and only service is redeployed, rather than the entire application from a change in numerous service changes. It is therefore advantageous over library components.

Decentralized Data Management

This is a common feature in most Microsystems and involves the centralization of conceptual models and data storage decisions. This feature has been praised by small business enterprises, since a single database stores data from essentially all applications. Furthermore, each service manages its own database through a technique called Polyglot Persistence. Decentralization of data is also key in managing data updates in microservices systems. This guarantees consistency when updating multiple resources. Microservices architecture requires transactionless coordination between services to ensure consistency, since distributed transactions may be difficult to implement. Inconsistency in data decentralization is prevented through compensating operations. However, this may be difficult to manage. Nonetheless, inconsistency in data decentralization should be present for a business to respond effectively to real-time demand for their products or services. The cost of fixing inconsistencies is less compared to the loss in a business experiencing great consistency in their data management systems.

Decentralized Governance

The microservices key feature is decentralized governance. The term governance means to control how people and solutions function to achieve organizational objectives. In SOA, governance guides the development of reusable service, developing and designing services, and establishing agreements between service providers and consumers. In microservices, architecture governance has the following capabilities;

- There is no need for central design governance since microservices can make their own decisions concerning its design and implementation

- Decentralized governance enables microservices to share common and reusable services

- Some of the run-time governance aspects, such as SLAs, throttling, security monitoring and service discovery, may be implemented at the API-GW level, which we are going to discuss later

Service Registry and Service Discovery

Microservices architecture entails dealing with numerous Microservices, which dynamically change in location owing to their rapid development/deployment nature. Therefore, to find their location during a runtime, service registry and discovery are essential.

Service registry holds the microservices instance and their location. Microservices instance is registered with the service registry on start-up and deregistered on shutdown. Clients can, therefore, find available services and their location through a service location

Service discovery is also used to find the location of available service. It uses two mechanisms, i.e. Client-Side Discovery and Service-Side Discovery

Advantages of Microservices

Microservices comes with numerous advantages, as discussed below:

- **Cost effective to scale**

You don't need to invest a lot to make the entire application scalable. In terms of a shopping cart, we could simply load balance the product search module and the order-processing module while leaving out less frequently used operation services, such as inventory management, order cancellation, and delivery confirmation.

- **Clear code boundaries**

This action should match an organization's departmental hierarchies. With different departments sponsoring product development in large enterprises, this can be a huge advantage.

- **Easier code changes**

The code is done in a way that it is not dependent on the code of other modules and is only achieving isolated functionality. If it is done right, the chances of a change in microservices affecting other microservices are very minimal.

- **Easy deployment:**

Since the entire application is more like a group of ecosystems that are isolated from each other, deployment could be done one microservices at a time, if required. Failure in any one of these would not bring the entire system down.

- **Technology adaptation**

You could port a single microservices or a whole bunch of them overnight to a different technology without your users even knowing about it. And yes, hopefully, you don't expect us to tell you that you need to maintain those service contracts, though.

- **Distributed system**

This comes as implied, but a word of caution is necessary here. Make sure that your asynchronous calls are used well, and synchronous ones are not really blocking the whole flow of information. Use data partitioning well. We will come to this a little later, so don't worry for now.

- **Quick market response**

The world being competitive is a definite advantage; otherwise, users tend to quickly lose interest if you are slow to respond to new feature requests or adoption of new technology within your system.

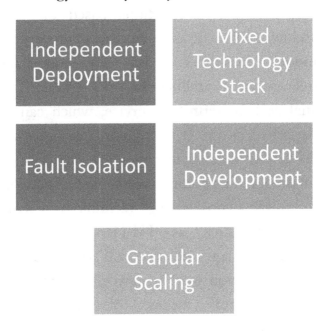

Advantages of Microservices

3. Understanding Microservices Architecture

Microservices have different methods of performing their functions based on their architectural style, as a standard microservices model does not exist. To understand microservices architecture, we should first analyze it in terms of service, which can be described as the basic unit in microservices. As briefly defined in chapter 1, Services are processes that communicate over a network to fulfil a goal using technology-agnostic protocols such as HTTP. Apart from technologic-agnostic protocols as a means of communication over a network, services also utilize other means of inter-process communication mechanisms, such as a shared memory for efficient communication over networks. Software developed through microservices architecture technique can be broken down into multiple component services. Each of the components in a service can be deployed, twisted according to the developer's specifications and then independently redeployed without having to develop an entirely new software application. However, this technique has its disadvantages, such as expensive remote calls, and complex procedures when redeploying and redistributing responsibilities between service components.

Services in microservices are organized around business capabilities such as user interface, front-end, recommendation, logistics, billing etc. The services in microservices can be implemented using different programming languages, databases, hardware, and software environments, depending on the developer's preferences. Microservices utilizes the cross-functional team, unlike a traditional monolith development approach where each team has a specific focus on technology layers, databases, Uls, server-side logic or technology layers. Each team in microservices is required to implement specific products based on one or more individual service communicating via a message bus. This improves the communicability of microservices over a network between a business enterprise and the end users of their products. While most software development technique focuses on handing a piece of code to the client and in turn maintained by a team, microservices employs the use of a team who owns a product for a lifetime.

A microservices based architecture adheres to principles such as fine-grained interface, business-driven development, IDEAL cloud application architectures, polyglot programming and lightweight container deployment and DevOps with holistic service monitoring to independently deploy services. To better our understanding of microservices, we can relate it to the classic UNIX system, i.e. they receive a user request, process them, and generate a response based on the query generated. Information flows in a microsystem through the dump pipes after being processed by smart endpoints.

Microservices entails numerous platforms and technologies to effectively execute their function. Microservices developers prefer to use decentralized governance over centralized governance, as it provides them with developing tools which can be used by other developers to solve emerging problems in software application development. Unlike microservices, monoliths systems utilize a single logical database across different platforms with each service managing its unique database.

The good thing about microservices is that it's a dynamic evolutionary software application technique in software application development. Therefore, it's an evolutionary design system which is ideal for the development of timeless applications which is compatible through future technologically sophisticated devices. In summary, Microservices functions by using services to componentized software applications, thereby ensuring efficient communication between applications and users over a network to fulfil an intended goal. The services are fine-grained and the protocols lightweight to break applications into small services to improve modularity and enable users to easily understand the functionality, development, and testing of the application software.

How Microservices Architecture Functions

Just like in programming, microservices have a wide range of functionality depending on the developer's choice. Microservices architecture functions by structuring applications into components or libraries of loosely coupled services, which are fine-grained and the protocols lightweight. But to understand its functionality, we should first look at Conway's law.

Conway's Law

A computer programmer named Melvin Conway came up a law in 1967 which states that "organizations which design system...are constrained to produce designs which are copies of the communication structure of these organization". This means that for a software module to function effectively there should be frequent communication between the authors. Social boundaries within an organization are reflected through the software interface structure within the application. Conway's law is the basic principle of the functionality of microservices and highlights the dangers of trying to enforce an application design that does not match the organizational requirements. To understand this, let's use an example: an organization having two departments i.e. accounting and customer support departments, whose application system are obviously interconnected. A problem arises that the accounting is overworked and cannot handle numerous tasks of processing both dissatisfied customer refunds and credit their accounts while the customer support department is underworked and very idle. How can the organization solve this problem? This is where microservices architecture comes in! The roles and responsibilities of each department in the interconnected system are split accordingly to improve customer satisfaction and minimize business losses in the organization.

In splitting the roles and responsibilities of each department, Interface Separation Principle is essential when implementing microservices to solve this problem. A typical approach isolating issues of concern in an organization through microservices is to find a communication point in the software application, then link the application by drawing a "dotted line" between the two halves of the system. However, this technique, if not carefully carried out, leads to smaller growing monoliths, which leads to isolation of important codes on the wrong side of the barrier.

Avoiding Monoliths in Microservices architecture application

Accidental monoliths are common problems when developing software applications using microservices architecture. An application may become infected with unhealthy interdependencies when service boundaries are blurred, and one service can start using the data source interface of another or even for code related to a certain logic or function to be spread over multiple places due to accidental monoliths which grow with time. This can be avoided by establishing the edge of developed application software graph.

Key Points in the Working of Microservices Architecture

- It is programming of the modern era, where we are expected to follow the SOLID principles. It's object-oriented programming (OOP).

- It is the best way to expose the functionality of other or external components in a way that any other programming language will be able to use the functionality without adhering to any specific user interfaces, that is, services (web services, APIs, rest services, and so on).

- The whole system works according to a

type of collaboration that is not interconnected or interdependent.

- Every component is liable for its own responsibilities. In other words, components are responsible for only one functionality.

- It segregates code with a separation concept, and the segregated code is reusable.

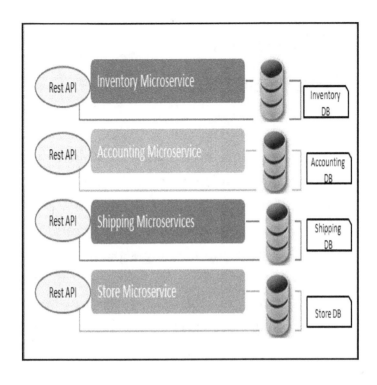

Microservices in Practice

4. Building Microservices

We have introduced and described the functionality of microservices. In this chapter, we are going to discuss how to build microservices by separating them from the existing system and creating separate services for products and orders which can be deployed independently. First, we will begin by discussing the core concepts, programming languages, and tools that can be used to build microservices.

- ***C#***

In 2002, Microsoft developed the C# programming language and the latest release is C# 7.0. C# is an object-oriented language and component oriented, with features like Deconstructors, ValueTuple, pattern matching, and much more.

- ### *Java Programming Language*

Java is a general-purpose programming language that is concurrent, class-based, object-oriented and designed to have few implementation dependencies as possible to let application developers "write once, run anywhere" (WORA), meaning that it can run on all platforms that support Java.

- ### *Entity Framework Core*

Entity framework core is a cross-platform version of the Microsoft Entity Framework and can be used as a tool to build microservices. It is one of the most popular object-relational mappers (ORMs). ORM can be defined as a technique to query and manipulate data as per the required business output.

- ### *.Net Framework*

Developed by Microsoft, NetFramework is a software framework that runs on Microsoft Windows with Framework Class Library to provide language interoperability across several programming languages. Programs are written for .NET Framework execute software environment, rather than hardware environment, or Common Language Runtime (CLR)

- ***Visual Studio 2017***

Visual Studio 2017 is an Integrated Development Environments (IDE) developed by Microsoft to enable software application developers to build applications using various programming languages, such as Java, C#, and many more.

- ***Microsoft SQL Server***

Microsoft SQL Server(MSSQL) is a software application that has a relational database software management system which is used to store and retrieve data as requested by other software applications. It can be used in the management of microservices and it is able to communicate across a network.

Aspects of Building

Microservices

To build microservices, we should first look at the important aspects, such as size and services to ensure their effective functionality after separating them from the main system.

Size of microservices

In building microservices, the first step is to break or decompose applications or systems into smaller segments or functionalities of the main application known as services. Factors to consider for high-level isolation of microservices are discussed below.

- **Risk due to requirement changes**

It is important to note that a change in one microservice should be independent of the other microservices. Therefore, software should be isolated into smaller components termed as services in a way that if there are any requirement changes in one service, they will be independent of other microservices.

- **Changes in Functionality**

In building microservices, we isolate functionalities that are rarely changed from the dependent functionalities that can be frequently modified. For example, in our application, the customer module notification functionality will rarely change. But its related modules, such as Order, are more likely to have frequent business changes as part of their life cycle.

- **Team changes**

We should also consider isolating modules in such a way that one team can work independently of all the other teams. If the process of making a new developer productive—regarding the tasks in such modules—is not dependent on people outside the team, it means we are well placed.

- **Technology changes**

Technology use needs to be isolated vertically within each module. A module should not be dependent on technology or component from another module. We should strictly isolate the modules developed in different technologies, or stacks, or look at moving them to a common platform as the last resort.

In building microservices, the primary goal is

to isolate services from the main application system and keep it as small as possible.

Features of a good Service

Good service is essential in the building of a good microservices architecture. A good service that can be easily used and maintained by developers and users should have the following characteristics.

- **Standard Data Formats**

Good service should follow standardized data formats while exchanging services or systems with other components. Most popular data formats used in the Netstack are XML and JSON

- **Standard communication protocol**

Good services should adhere to standard communication formats such as SOAP and REST

- **Loose coupling**

Coupling refers to the degree of direct knowledge that one service has of another. Therefore, loosely coupled means that they should not have little knowledge of the other service so that a change in one service will not impact the other service.

Domain -Driven Design in building Microservices

Domain-Driven Design (DDD) is a technique in designing complex systems and can be useful in designing and building microservices. DDD can be described as a blueprint used to build microservices and, once it's done, a microservices can implement it just the way an application implements, let's say, an order service or an inventory service. The main principle in domain design is to draft a model which can be written in any programming language after understanding an exact domain problem. A domain is driven model should be reusable, loosely coupled, independently designed, and should be easily isolated from a software application without having to deploy a new system.

After building microservices from a domain-based model, it is important to ensure that the size of the microservices is small enough.

This can be done by having a baseline for the maximum number of domain objects which can communicate with each other. You can also do this by verifying the size of all interfaces and classes in each microservices. Another way of ensuring a small size of microservices is by achieving the correct vertical isolation of services. You can then deploy each of the services independently. By deploying each service independently, we allow the host in an application to perform its independent process which is beneficial in harnessing the power of the cloud and other hybrid models of hosting.

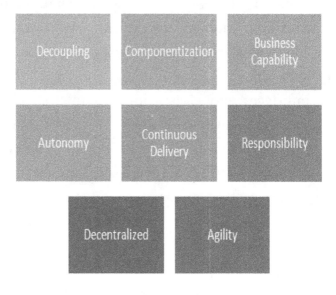

Microservices Features

Building Microservices from Monolithic Application

As discussed earlier, the functionality in microservices lies in the isolation of services from the rest of the application system translating into advantages discussed in chapter 1such as code reusability, independent deployment and easier code maintenance. Building microservices from monolithic application needs thorough planning. Many software architects have different approaches when it comes to transiting from monoliths to microservices, but the most important thing to consider is a correct method, as there is a possibility microservices failing to carry out their function when translated from monolith application using a wrong method. Some of the factors to consider when building microservices from the monolithic application are discussed below:

- **Module interdependency**

When building microservices from the monolithic application, the starting point should always be to identify and pick up those parts of the monolithic application that are least dependent on other modules and have the least dependent on them. This part of the application is essential in identifying isolating application codes from the rest of the system, thereby becoming a part of the microservices which are then deployed independently in the final stage of the process. This small part of the application is referred to as seams.

- **Technology**

Technology in the form of an application's

base framework is important in achieving this process. Before choosing a software framework, such as the ones discussed in this chapter, you should first identify their features. Building microservices is heavily dependent on data structures, inter-process communication is performed, and the activity of report generation. In this regard, a developer should, therefore, choose a framework that has great features and is ahead in technology, as they enable them to perform the transition correctly

- **Team structure**

Team structure is important in the transition, as they are the workforce in building microservices. Teams greatly differ based on the geographical location, security of the company, and their technical skills. For the team to optimize their productivity in building microservices, they should be able to work independently. Furthermore, the team should safeguard the intellectual property of the company in developing a microservices based application.

- **Database**

The database is considered the biggest asset of a system and their domain is defined by database tables and stored procedure. Contrary to most misconceptions, building microservices from the monolithic application does not involve dividing the whole database at once, but rather a step-by-step procedure. First, a database structure used to interact with the database is identified. Then the database structure is isolated into separate codes, which are then aligned with the newly defined vertical boundaries. Secondly, the underlying database structure is broken using the same method as the first step. The database change should not define the module used in the transition to microservices-style architecture, but rather the module should define the database. The database structure should relate to the modules picked in the transition to ensure ease in building microservices.

It is important to understand the types of acceptable changes in breaking down and merging a database, as not all changes can be implemented by the system due to data integrity. When restructuring a database to match the microservices architecture, removing foreign key relationship is the most important step, as microservices are designed to function independently of other services in an application. The final step in breaking database in microservices-style architecture is isolating the ORDER table from the ProductID, as they are still sharing information, i.e. loose coupling.

In summary, breaking down a database in a microservices architecture style involves two important steps: Isolating the data structures in the code and removing foreign key relationships. It is important to note that splitting the database is not the final step in building microservices from monolithic applications, as there are other steps.

- **Transaction**

After splitting the database from the steps mentioned above, the next step is to link services to the database in a way that ensures data integrity is maintained. However, not all services successfully go through a transaction to their successful databases due to several reasons, such as a communication fault within the system or insufficient quantities for the product requested in e-commerce platforms. For example, Amazon and e-commerce. These problems can be solved by orchestrating the whole transaction, record individual transactions across the service, or to cancel the entire transaction across the services in the system. However, when the transactions are planned out well in a microservices-style architecture application, this problem can be avoided

Building Microservices with Java

Building microservices in a java ecosystem includes container-less, self-contained and in-container strategies, all of which are discussed below.

- **Container-less microservices**

Container-less microservices package the application, with all of its dependencies, into a single JAR file. This approach is very advantageous, due to the ease of starting and stopping services as necessary in scaling. A JAR file is also conveniently passed around by the team members that need it.

• Self-contained microservices

Like container-fewer microservices, microservices are packaged into a single fat JAR file with the inclusion of embedded framework with optional compatible third-party libraries, such as Wildfly Swarm and Spring Boot, both of which will be discussed later in this chapter.

• In-Container microservices

In-container microservices package an entire Java EE container and its service implementation in a Docker image. The container provides verified implementations through standard APIs, giving the developer the opportunity to solely focus on business functionality.

Microservices Framework for Java

Apart from the containers discussed above, building microservices in Java entails several microservices frameworks, such as Spring

Boot, Jersey, Swagger, Dropwizard, Ninja Web Framework, Play Framework, and many more. We are going to handle just a few common microservices frameworks below.

• **Microservices in Spring Boot**

Spring Boot is one of the best microservices frameworks since it is optimally integrated with supporting languages. You can Spring Boot on your own device via an embedded server. Spring Boot also eliminates the necessity of using Java EE containers. This is enabled through the implementation of Tomcat. Spring boot projects include:

• **Spring IO Platform:**

An enterprise-grade distribution for versioned applications.

• **Spring Framework:**

Used for transaction management, data access, dependency injection, messaging, and web apps.

• **Spring Cloud:**

Used for distributed systems and also used

for building or deploying your microservices.

- **Spring Data:**

Used for microservices that are related to data access, be it map-reduce, relational or even non-relational.

- **Spring Batch:**

Used for higher levels of batch operations.

- **Spring Security:**

Used for authorization and authentication support.

- **Spring REST Docs:**

Used for documenting RESTful services.

- **Spring Social:**

Used for connecting to social media APIs.

- **Spring Mobile:**

Used for mobile Web apps.

- **Microservices in Dropwizard**

Dropwizard combines mature and stable Java libraries in lightweight packages for use in a certain application. It uses Jetty for HTTP,

Jersey for REST, and Jackson for JSON, along with Metrics, Guava, Logback, Hibernate Validator, Apache HTTP Client, Liquibase, Mustache, Joda Time, and Freemarker. Maven is used to setting up Dropbox application, after which a configuration class, an application class, a representation class, a resource class, or a health check can be created to run the applications.

- **Jersey**

Jersey is an open source framework based on JAX-RS specifications. Jersey's applications can extend existing JAX-RS implementations with more features and utilities to make RESTful services and client development simpler and easier. Jersey is fast and easily routed, coupled with great documentation filled with examples for easy practice.

- **Play Framework**

Play Framework provides an easier way to build, create, and deploy Web applications using Scala and Java. It is ideal for REST application that requires parallel handling of remote calls. It is one of the most used microservices frameworks with modular and supports async. An example of code in Play Framework is shown below.

- **Restlet**

Restlet enables developers to create fast and scalable WEB APIs that adhere to the RESTful architecture pattern discussed above. It has good routing and filtering, and it's available for Java SE/EE, OSGi, Google AppEngine, Android, and other major platforms. However, learning Restlet can be difficult due to the small number of users and the unavailability of tutorials. An example of a code in Restlet is shown below.

5. Integrating Microservices

Integrating microservices refers to interaction and communication of independent services located in a separate database within a software application. First, let us look at communication between microservices.

Communication between Microservices

Microservices communicate using an inter-process communication mechanism with two main message formats, namely binary and text. There are two kinds of inter-process communication mechanisms that microservices can be used to communicate, i.e. asynchronous messaging and synchronous request/response, both of which are discussed below.

Asynchronous Communication

This is an inter-process communication mechanism in which microservices communicate by asynchronously exchanging messages. It means that when an organizational client sends a message to a service to perform a certain task or answer a query, the service replies by sending a separate message back to the client. The messages, consisting of a title and body, are exchanged over channels with no limitation to the number of organizations and their clients sending and receiving messages. Likewise, any number of consumers can receive multiple messages from a single communication channel. There are two types of channels, namely: publish-subscribe and point-to-point channels. A point-to-point channel delivers a message to exactly one client reading from the channel, while the publish-subscribe channel delivers a common message to all the attached clients in a certain organization. Services utilize point-to-point channel to communicate directly to clients and publish-subscribe communication to interact with one too many clients attached to an organization

For instance, when a client requests a trip through an application, The Trip Management is notified and in turn, notifies the Dispatch department about the new trip through a Trip Created message to a publish-subscribe channel. The Dispatcher then locates an available driver and notifies them by writing a Driver Proposed message to a publish-subscribe channel.

Some of the advantages of this type of communication include message buffering, isolating the client from the service, flexibility in client-service interactions, and explicitly in inter-process communication. However, there are certain downsides, such as additional operational costs, since the system is a separate entity and must be installed, configured, and operated separately, and the complexity of implementing request/response-based interaction.

Synchronous, Request/Response IPC Mechanism

In this inter-process mechanism, a client sends a request to a service, which in turn processes the request and sends back a response. The client believes that the response will arrive in a timely fashion. While using synchronous IPC mechanism, one can choose various protocols to choose from, but the most common ones are REST and Thrift, as discussed below.

REST

REST is an IPC mechanism that uses HTTP to communicate. The basic in REST is a resource which can be equated to a business entity, such as a product or a customer or a collection of business objects. REST utilizes HTTP verbs referenced using a URL to manipulate resources. The key benefit of using this protocol is that it's simple and familiar and supports request/response-style communication, thereby enabling real-time communication within an organization and numerous clients. Some of the drawbacks include that the intermediary and buffer messages must all run concurrently and that the client must know the location of each service through a URL.

Thrift

An alternative to REST is the Apache Thrift, which provides a C-style IDL for defining APIs. Thrift is essential in generating client-side stubs and server-side skeletons. A thrift interface is made up of one or more services, which can return a value to implement the request/response style of interaction. Thrift also supports various message formats such, as JSON, binary, and compact binary.

Integration Patterns

We have discussed communication between microservices through synchronous and asynchronous inter-process communication, but this alone does not guarantee integration, as integration patterns are also essential in their communication. We will discuss the implementation of various integration patterns required by an application. The API Gateway

The API gateway sits between clients and services by acting as a reverse proxy, routing requests from clients to services. It acts as a proxy between services and client applications. The Azure API management as an example is responsible for the following functionalities.

- Accepting API calls

- Verifying API keys, JWT tokens, and certificates

- Supporting Auth through Azure AD and OAuth 2.0 access token

- Enforcing usage quotas and rate limits

- Caching backend responses

- Logging call metadata for analytics purposes

To understand the integration of microservices in Azure API gateway, let's use an example of an application split into microservices, namely product service, order service, invoice service, and customer service. In this application, the Azure API will be working as an API Gateway to connect clients to services. The API gateway enables clients to access services in servers unknown to them by providing its own server address and authenticating the client's request by using a valid Ocp-Apim-Subscription-Key

Different API commands execute certain functions in service, as shown in the table below:

API Resource	Description
GET /api/product	Gets a list of products
GET /api/product/{id}	Gets a product
PUT /api/product/{id}	Updates an existing product
DELETE	Deletes an

/api/product/{id}	existing product
POST /api/product	Adds a new product

The Event-Driven pattern

A microservice has a database per service pattern, meaning that it has an independent database for every dependent or independent service. Dependent services require a few external services or components, and internal services to function effectively. Dependent service does not work if any or all the services on which the service is dependent on do not work properly. Independent service does not require any other service to work properly, as the name suggests.

In the diagram, the event-manager could be a program which runs on a service which enables it to manage all the events of the subscribers. Whenever a specific event is triggered in the Publisher, the event-manager notifies a Subscriber.

Event Sourcing

Event sourcing pattern enables developers to publish an event whenever the state changes. The EventStore persists the events available for subscription, or as other services. In this pattern, tasks are simplified to avoid additional requirements in synchronizing the data model and business domain, thereby improving responsiveness, scalability, and responsiveness in the microservices. For example, in an application having ORDERSERVICE as the services, a command issues a book for the User Interface to be ordered. ORDERSERVICE queries and populates the results with the `CreateOrder` event from the Event Store. The command handler raises an event to order the book, initiating a related operation. Finally, the system authorizes the event by appending the event to the event store.

Compensating Transactions

Compensating transactions refers to a means used to undo tasks performed in a series of steps. For instance, a service has implemented operations in a series and one or more tasks have failed. Compensating transactions is used to reverse the steps in a series.

Competing Consumers

Competing consumers is essential in processing messages for multiple concurrent consumers to receive messages on the same channel. It enables an application to handle numerous requests from clients. It is implemented by passing a messaging system to another service through asynchronous communication.

Azure Service Bus

Azure Service Bus is an information delivery service used to enhance communication between two or more services. Azure Service Bus can be described as a means through which services communicate or exchange information. Azure Service Bus provides two main types of service, which are broken and non-broken communication. Broken communication is a real-time communication that ensures communication between a sender or a receiver, even when they are offline. In non-broken communication, the sender is not informed whether information has been received or not by the receiver.

Azure queues

Azure queues are cloud storage accounts which use Azure Table. They provide a means to queue a message between applications. In summary, integrating microservices is through communication between services. Microservices communicate through inter-service communication, which can be synchronous or asynchronous. In asynchronous inter-process communication, API gateway is used to allow clients to communicate to services by acting as an intermediary between clients and services. Microservices also communicate through various patterns, as discussed in the chapter.

Chapter 6: Testing Microservices

Testing microservices is an important way of ensuring their functionality by assessing the system, applications, or programs in different aspects to identify an erroneous code. Testing microservices varies in systems, depending on the microservices architectural style employed.

How to Test Microservices

It is easier to test a monolithic application than to test microservices since monoliths provide implementation dependencies and short note delivery cycles. This is because testing microservices involves testing each service separately, with the test technique different for each service. Testing microservices can be challenging since each service is designed to work independently. Therefore, they are tested individually rather than as a whole system It gets more challenging when testing is combined with continuous integration and deployment. However, these challenges can be solved by using a unit test framework. For example, Microsoft Unit Testing Framework, which provides a facility to test individual operations of independent components. These tests are run on every compilation of the code to ensure success in the test.

Testing Approach

As mentioned above, different application systems require different testing approaches. The testing strategy should be unique to a system and should be clear to everyone, including the none technical members of a team. Testing can be manual or automated and should be simple to perform by a system user. Testing approaches have the following techniques.

- **Proactive Testing**

A testing approach that tries to fix defects before a build is created from the initial test designs

- **Reactive Testing**

Testing is started after the completion of coding.

- **Testing Pyramid**

To illustrate testing microservices, we use the testing pyramid. The Testing pyramid showcases how a well-designed test strategy is structured.

- **Testing Pyramid:**

- System Tests (Top)

- Service Tests (Middle)

- Unit Tests (Bottom)

- **Unit Test**

Unit testing involves testing small functionalities of an application based on the microservices architectural style.

- **Service Tests**

Service tests entail testing an independent service which communicates with another/external service

- **System Tests**

They are end-to-end tests, useful in testing the entire system with an aspect of the user interface. System tests are expensive and slow to maintain and write, while service and unit tests are fast and less expensive.

Types of Microservices Test

There are various types of microservices test, as discussed below.

- **Unit Testing**

Unit testing is used to test a single function in service, thereby ensuring that the smallest piece of the program is tested. They are carried out to verify a specific functionality in a system without having to test other components in the process. Unit testing is very complex since the components are broken down into independent, small components that can be tested independently. Test-Driven Development is used to perform a unit test.

- **Component (service) Testing**

In service testing, the units(UI) are directly

bypassed and the API, suchas.Net Core Web API is tested directly. Testing a service involves testing an independent service or a service interacting with an external device. A mock and stub approach is used to test a service interacting with an external service through an API gateway.

- **Integration Testing**

Integration testing involves testing services in components working together. It is meant to ensure that the system is working together correctly as expected. For example, an application has StockService and OrderService depending on each other. Using integration testing, StockService is tested individually by ensuring it does not communicate with OrderService. This is accomplished through mock.

- **Contract Testing**

Contract testing is a test that involves verifying response in each independent service. In this test, any service that is dependent on an external service is stubbed, therefore making it function independently.

This test is essential in checking the contract of external services through a consumer-driven contract, as discussed below.

• Consumer-driven contracts

Consumer-driven refers to an integration pattern, which specifies and verifies interactions between clients and the application through the API gateway. It specifies the type of interactions a client is requesting with a defined format. The applications can then approve the requests through consumer-driven contract.

• Performance Testing

It is non-functional testing with the aim of ensuring the system is performing perfectly according to its features, such as scalability and reliability. Performance testing involves various techniques, as described below.

• Load Testing

This technique involves testing the behaviour of the application system under various conditions of a specific load, such as database load, critical transactions, and application servers

- **Stress Testing**

It is a test where the system is exposed to regress stressing to find the upper capacity of the system. It is aimed at determining the behaviour of a system in critical conditions, such as when the current load overrides the maximum load.

- **Soak Testing**

Also called endurance testing, soak testing is aimed at monitoring memory utilization, memory leaks, and other factors influencing system performance

- **Spike Testing**

Spike testing is an approach in which the system is tested to ensure it can sustain the workload. It can be done by suddenly increasing the workload and monitoring system performance

- **End-to-end (UI/functional) testing**

UI test is performed on the whole system,

including the entire service and database. This test is the highest level of testing in microservices and it's mainly performed to increase the scope of testing. It includes fronted integration.

- ## Sociable versus isolated unit Tests

Sociable tests resemble system tests and are performed to ensure that the application is running smoothly and as expected. Additionally, it tests other software in the same application environment. Isolated software, on the other hand, is performed before stubbing and mocking to perform unit testing, as discussed earlier. Unit testing can also be used to perform using stubs in a concrete class

- ## Stubs and Mocks

Stubs and mocks are the mock implementations of objects interacting with the code when performing a test. The object can be replaced with a stub in one test and a mock on the other, depending on the intention of the test. Stubs can be referred to as inputs to the code under test, while mocks are outputs of code under test

Summary

We have discussed that testing microservices is more challenging compared to testing monolithic applications in the a.Net framework. The pyramid test concept enables us to understand and strategize testing procedures. A unit test is used in testing small functionalities and class in a microservices application. Tests on top of the pyramid, such as end-end testing, are used to test the entire microservices application, rather than small functionalities or services in the application.

Chapter 7: Deploying Microservices

Microservices can also be challenging and is done through continuous integration and continuous deployment. Additionally, new technology such as tool chain technology and container technologies have proven essential in deploying microservices. In this chapter, we are going to discuss the basics of microservices deployment and the new technologies mentioned above. But first, let's look at the key requirements in their deployment.

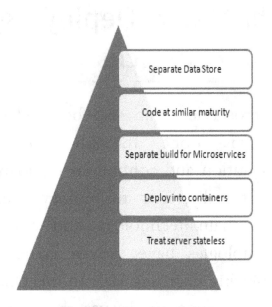

Microservices Best Practices

Deployment Requirement

- Ability to deploy/un-deploy services independent of other microservices

- A service must be able to, at each microservices level, ensure a given service does not receive more traffic compared to other services in the application.

- A failure in one microservices must not

affect other services in the application

- Building and deploying microservices quickly

Steps in Microservices Deployment

In this section, we are going to discuss the first step, i.e. Build to the final stage, which is the release stage.

- **Build Stage**

In the build stage, a docker container is made to provide the necessary tools to create the microservices. A second container is then applied to run the built container. Then, a service source is compiled carefully to prevent errors. The services are later tested using unit testing to ensure their correspondence. The final product in this stage is a build artefact.

- **Continuous Integration (CI)**

Any changes in the microservices build the entire application through CI. This occurs because the application code gets compiled and a comprehensive set of automated tests are run against it. CI was developed due to the problem of frequent integration. The basic idea behind CI is to ensure small changes in the software application by preserving a Delta.

• Deployment

Requirements for deployment include the hardware specifications, base OS, and the correct version of a software framework. The final part is to promote the build artifacts produced in the first stage. In microservices, there is a distinction between the deployment stage and the release stage.

• Continuous Deployment (CD)

In this stage, each build is deployed to the production. It is important in the deployment of microservices, as it ensures that the changes pushed to production through various lower environment work as expected in the production. This stage involves several practices, such as automated unit testing, labeling, versioning of build numbers, and traceability of changes.

• Continuous Delivery

Continuous delivery is different from

continuous deployment(CD) and it's focused on providing the deployment code as early as possible to the customer. In Continuous Delivery, every build is passed through quality checks to prevent errors. Continuous Delivery is implemented through automation by the build and deployment pipeline. Build and deployment pipelines ensure that a code is committed in the source repository.

- **Release**

This is the final stage in microservices deployment and involves making a service available to possible clients. The relevant build artifact is deployed before the release of a service managed by a toggle.

Fundamentals for Successful Microservices Deployment

For microservices to be deployed successfully, the following things should be done.

- **Self-sufficient Teams**

A team should have sufficient members with all the necessary skills and roles i.e. developers and analysts. A self-sufficient team will be able to handle the development, operations, and management of microservices effectively. Smaller self-sufficient teams, who can integrate their work frequently, are precursors to the success of microservices.

- **CI and CD**

CI and CD are essential in implementing microservices, as they automate the system to be able to push code upgrades regularly, thereby enabling the team to handle complexity by deploying microservices, as discussed above.

- **Infrastructure Coding**

Infrastructure coding refers to representing hardware and infrastructure components, such as network servers into codes. It is important to provide deployment environments to make integration, testing, and build production possible in microservices production. It also enables developers to produce defects in lower environments. Tools such as CFEngine, Chef, Puppet, Ansible and PowerShell DSC can be used to code infrastructure. Through infrastructure coding, an infrastructure can be put under a version control system, then deployed as an artifact to enhance microservices deployment.

- **Utilization of Cloud Computing**

Cloud computing is important in the adoption and deployment of microservices. It comes with near infinite scale, elasticity, and rapid provision capability. Therefore, it should be utilized to ensure the successful deployment of microservices.

- **Deploying Isolated Microservices**

In 2012, Adam Wiggins developed a set of principles known as a 12-factor app, which can be used to deploy microservices. According to the principles, the services are essentially stateless except for the database. These principles are applied in deploying isolated microservices as follows.

- **Service teams**

The team should be self-sufficient and built around services. They should be able to make the right decision to develop and support the microservices decision.

- **Source control isolation**

Source control isolation ensures that microservices do not share any source code or files in their respiratory. However, codes can be duplicated to avoid this problem.

- **Build Stage Isolation**

Build and deploy pipelines for microservices should be isolated and separate. For isolated deployed services, build and deploy pipelines run separately. Due to this, the CI-CD tool is scaled to support different services and pipelines at a faster stage.

- **Release Stage Isolation**

Every microservice is released in isolation with other services.

- **Deploy Stage Isolation**

It is the most important stage in deploying isolated microservices.

Containers

Containers can be defined as pieces of software in a complete file system. Container technology is new and is now linked to the Linux world. Containers are essential in running code, runtime, system tools, and system libraries. They share their host operating system and kernel with other containers on the same host.

Deploying Microservices with Docker.

Docker is an open-source engine that lets developers and system administrators deploy self-sufficient application containers (defined above) in the Linux environment. It is a great way to deploy microservices. The building deploying when starting microservices is much faster when using the Docker platform. Deploying microservices using docker is performed by following these simple steps.

- The microservices is packaged as a Docker container image

- Each service is deployed as a container

- Scaling is done based on changing the number of container instances.

Terminologies used in Docker

Docker image

A Docker image is a read-only template containing instructions for creating a Docker container. It consists of a separate file system, associated libraries, and so on. It can be composed of layers on top each other, like a layered cake. Docker images used in different containers can be reused, thereby reducing the deployment footprints of applications using the same images. A Docker image can be stored at the Docker hub.

Docker registry

Docker registry is a library of images and can either be private or public. It can also be on the same server as the Docker daemon or Docker client, or on a totally different server.

Dockerfile

A Dockerfile is a scripted file containing instructions on how to build a Docker image.

The instructions are in the form of multiple steps, starting from obtaining the base image.

Docker Container

Refers to a runnable instance of a Docker image.

Docker Compose

It enables a developer to define application components i.e. containers, configuration, links, volumes in a single service. A single command is then executed to establish every component in the application and run the application.

Docker Swarm

It's a Docker service in which container nodes function together. It operates as a defined number of instances of a replica task in a Docker image.

Deploying Microservices with Kubernetes

Kubernetes is a recent technology in deploying microservices. It extends Docker capabilities since Linux containers can be managed in a single system. It also allows the management and running of Docker containers across multiple hosts offering co-location of containers, service discovery, and replication control. Kubernetes has become an extremely powerful approach in deploying microservices, especially for large-scale microservices deployments.

Summary

We have discussed that for microservices to be deployed effectively, developers should adhere to the best deployment practices, as discussed in this chapter.

they isolate services. Microservices can be deployed using either Docker or Kubernetes, as discussed above.

Chapter 8: Security in Microservices

Securing microservices is a requirement for an enterprise running their applications or websites on microservices since data breaches or hacking are very common these days and can lead to massive unwarranted loses. As much as security in an organization is everyone's responsibility, microservices should be secured after their deployment, as we are going to discuss in this chapter. First, let's look at security in monolithic applications.

Security in Monolithic Applications

As we discussed earlier, monolithic applications are deployed dependently, whereby they have a large surface area in an application compared to microservices. The fact that microservices are isolated from each other and deployed independently means that they are more secure, compared to monoliths. However, implementing security in microservices can be challenging. The monolithic application has different attack vectors from microservices, and its security is implemented as follows.

- Security in a typical monolithic application is about finding 'who is the intruder' and 'what can they do' and how do we propagate the information.

- After establishing this information, security is then implemented from a common security component which is at the beginning of the request handling chain. The component uses an underlying user respiratory or a store to populate the required information.

This is done through an authentication (auth) mechanism, which verifies the identity of a user and manages what they can or cannot access through permissions. Data from the client to the server is then secured through encryption achieved through the HTTPS protocol. In an a.Net monolithic application, a user files a request to a web application through a web browser which requires them to enter their username and password. This request is then transferred through HTTPS and load balancer to the Auth, which then connects to the user credential store container, such as SQL server, which contains login details of various users. The user-supplied credentials i.e. username and password, are then verified against the ones retrieved from credentials store by the auth layer.

On verification, the user's browser automatically creates a cookie session, enabling him or her to access the requested information. In this kind of monolithic application, security is achieved by ensuring that the application modules do not separate verification and validation of request while communicating with each other.

Security in Microservices

Security in microservices architecture is achieved by translating the pattern used in securing monolithic applications to microservices. In microservices, the authentication layer is broken into microservices in different applications, which will need its authentication mechanisms. The user credential store is different for every microservices. From our previous discussion, this pattern cannot be implemented, since auth cannot be synced across all devices, and validating inter-process communication might be impossible. Additionally, modern applications based on Android or iOS cannot support secure information between clients and services, since session-based authentication using cookies is not possible, as in monolithic applications. So, the question is how these problems are solved to secure microservices application. The solution comes in the form of OpenID Connect, JSON Web Tokens and OAuth 2.0, as we will discuss below.

JSON Web Tokens

JSON Web Tokens(JWT) is used in producing a data structure which contains information about the issuer and the recipient, along with the sender's identity. They can be deployed independently, irrespective of OAuth 2.0 or OpenID Connect, as they are not tied together. The tokens are secured with symmetric and asymmetric keys to ensure information received by a client is authentic or trustable.

The OAuth 2.0

The OAuth 2.0 is an authorization framework that lets a third-party application to obtain finite access to an HTTP service, either on behalf of the resource owner by orchestrating an approval interaction between the resource owner and the HTTP servic or by allowing the third-party application to obtain access on its behalf. OAuth 2.0 functions as a delegated authorization framework, relying on authentication mechanisms to complete the authorization framework. The figure below illustrates the functionality of OAuth in securing microservices.

OpenID Connect

It comes top of OAuth 2.0 protocol and its importance in the user authentication i.e. standard for authentication. It allows a client to verify end users based on the authentication performed by an authorization server. It is also used to obtain the basic profile information of end users. Clients using any device, i.e. web-based, mobile and javascript can access information relating to authenticated sessions and end users through OpenID Connect. Validation of the end user is through sending ID token to an application used by a client.

To understand microservices security, let's use an example of a client requesting service through his/ her mobile-based microservices application. OAuth and the OpenID Connect (Authorization Server) authenticate the client to access data in the microservices by issuing the Access Token. The API Gateway is the only entry to the application's microservices, and then receives the Access Token along with the client's request. The Token Translation at the API Gateway extracts the Access token from the client's request and sends it to the authorization server to retrieve the JSON Web Tokens. JSON tokens, along with the client's request, are then passed to the microservices layer by the API Gateway. JSON Web Token contains the necessary information used in storing user sessions. At each microservices layer, there are components used to process the JSON tokens, thereby obtaining the client's request and its information.

Other Security Practices

There are other practices to secure microservices apart from OAuth 2.0 and Open ID connect, as we are going to discuss below.

Standardization of libraries and frameworks

This refers to introducing libraries and frameworks in the development process. It is done to ease out patching, in case of any vulnerability found. It also minimizes the risk introduced by ad hoc implementation of libraries or tools around development.

Regular vulnerability Identification and mitigation

The vulnerability is regularly checked using an industry-standard vulnerability scanner to scan the source code, coupled with binaries and the findings addressed accordingly.

Third-party audits and penetration testing

External audits and penetration test are conducted regularly as they are essential in ensuring data integrity in applications or websites involving sensitive critical data or information

Logging and monitoring

Logging is useful in detecting and recovering from hacking attacks by aggregating logs from different systems and services, thereby essential in microservices security

Network Segregation

Network segregation or partitioning, although only possible in the monolithic application, can be effective in ensuring the security of microservices. This can be achieved through the creation of different network segments and subnets.

Summary

We have discussed that securing microservices is essential to any organization having microservices application systems. Security patterns in a monolithic application cannot be implemented in microservices application due to incompatibility problems, such as each microservices requiring their own authentication mechanism and so on, as discussed in this chapter. Therefore, secure token-based approaches such as OAuth 2.0 and OpenID Connect can be used to secure microservices through authorization and authentication.

Chapter 9: Criticism and Case Study

The emergence of microservices as a technique in software application development has been largely criticized for some reasons, namely:

- Information barriers due to services

- Communication of services over a network is costly in terms of network latency and message processing time

- Complexity in testing and deployment

- Difficulty in moving responsibilities between services. It involves communication between different teams, rewriting the functionality in another language or fitting it into a different infrastructure.

- Too many services, if not deployed correctly, may slow system performance.

- Additional complexity, such as network latency, message formats, load balancing and fault tolerance.

Nano service

Nano service refers to anti-patterns where a service is too fine-grained, meaning that the overheads outweighs its utility. Microservices have continually been criticized as a Nano service due to numerous problems such as the code overhead, runtime overhead, and fragmented logic. However, there are some proposed alternatives to the Nano service. These are:

- Packaging the functionality as a software library rather than a service.

- Combining the functionality with other functionalities to produce a more substantial useful service

- Refactoring the system by putting the functionality in other services or redesigning the system altogether.

Design for Failure

Microservices have been criticized as prone to failure compared to monolith since they introduce isolated services to the system, which increases the possibility of having a system failure. Some of the reasons that may lead to failure in microservices include network instability and unavailability of the underlying resources. However, there are certain design mechanisms that may ensure an unavailable or unresponsive microservices does not cause the whole application to fail. It ensures that microservices is fault tolerant and swiftly recovers after experiencing a failure. In microservices, it is important to maintain real-time monitoring, since services can fail at any time. The failures should be repaired quickly to be able to restore the services. Let's discuss common ways of avoiding failure in microservices application.

Circuit Breaker

A circuit breaker is a fault monitor component which is configured to each service in the application. The fault monitor then observes service failures, and when they reach a certain threshold, the circuit breaker stops any further requests to the services. This is essential in avoiding unnecessary resource consumption by requesting delay timeouts. It is also important in monitoring the whole system.

Bulkhead

Since microservices applications comprise of numerous services, a failure in one service may affect the functioning of other microservices or even the entire application. Bulkhead is essential in preventing a failure in one microservices from affecting the whole application, as it isolates different parts of the microservices application

Timeout

Timeout is a pattern mechanism to prevent clients from over waiting for a response from microservices once they have sent as a request through there devices. Clients configure a time interval in which they are comfortable to wait for increasing efficiency and client satisfaction.

These patterns are configured to the API Gateway and monitor the response of the microservices once they receive a request. When a service is unresponsive or unavailable, the Timeout mechanism notifies the user to try accessing the microservices another time to avoid overloading the application system and prevent failure in one service from affecting the other microservices. Additionally, the Gateway can be used as the central point to monitor each microservices, thereby informing developers of a failure.

Microservices Disrupting the Fintech Industries

Microservices have greatly disrupted the Fintech industries and other sectors. By breaking down big, complex systems into smaller pieces or services, microservices allow complicated work to be divided and distributed amongst smaller teams, making it easier to develop, test and deploy. Fintech industries are realizing that they are being disrupted and need to reinvent them to compete against these digital-only businesses.

The speed of innovation is dictated by the ability to expose business assets in a digital-friendly manner, and in some instances leverage external assets to provide a more social experience. The core paradigm enabling the use of business assets within mobile or tablet applications is through microservices. For a large majority of enterprises, microservices have become a new business channel to expose key assets, data, or services for consumption by mobile, web, internet of things, and enterprise applications. It can represent monetary benefit by metering usage of API services and providing different plans (i.e. Gold, Silver Bronze) at various price-points, or simply making them available at no-charge to increase usage and brand promotion through increased marketing.

Companies using Microservices

Chapter 10: Summary

We have discussed a lot about microservices from their invention, definition, advantages, building, integration techniques, deployment, and finally their security. In this chapter, we are going to recap what we have already discussed.

Before Microservices?

As we had discussed, before the invention of microservices, monolithic architecture and Service-Oriented Architecture was used to develop software applications

Monolithic Architecture

The monolithic architecture consists of components such as user interface, business logic, and database access, which are interconnected and interdependent. Therefore, a minor change in any module of the application results in a change to the entire application. This would require the redeployment of the entire application. Monolithic architecture has numerous challenges, including code complexity, scalability, large interdependent code, and difficulty in the adoption of new technology in terms of application or new devices.

Service-oriented architecture

Service-oriented architecture is an improvement of monolithic architecture resolving some of the challenges we mentioned above. Services primarily started with SOA and it's the main concept behind it. As we have already defined, a service is a piece of program or code providing some functionality to the system components. SOA comes with some advantages, such as the ability to reuse codes, and the ability to upgrade applications without necessarily deploying the entire application.

Microservices architecture

Microservices architecture is very similar to SOA, except that services are deployed independently. A change in a piece of program or code does not change the functionality of the entire application. For services to function independently, a certain discipline and strategy are required. Some of the disadvantages we discussed include clear boundaries, easy deployment, technology adaptation, affordable scalability, and quick market response.

Building Microservices from Monoliths

We discussed building microservices from an existing monolithic application. First is to identify decomposition candidates within a monolith based on parameters including code complexity, technology adaptation, resource requirement, and human dependency. Second is the identification of seams, which act as boundaries in microservices, then the separation can start. Seams should be picked on the right parameters depending on module interdependency, team structure, database. and existing technology. The master database should be handled with care through a separate service or configuration. An advantage of microservices having its own database is that it removes many of the existing foreign key relationships, thereby has a high transaction-handling ability.

Integration Techniques

Microservices integration techniques are mainly based on communication between microservices. We discussed that there are two ways in which microservices communicate: synchronous and asynchronous communication. Synchronous communication is based on request/response, while the asynchronous style is event-based. Integration patterns are essential to facilitate complex interaction among microservices. We discussed integrating microservices using event-driven patterns in the API Gateway. The event-driven pattern works by some services publishing their events, and some subscribing to those available events. The subscribing services simply react independently to the event-publishing services, based on the event and its metadata.

Deployment

We discussed microservices deployment and how it can be challenging for various reasons. Breaking the central database further increases the overall challenges. Microservices deployment requires continuous delivery(CD) and continuous integration (CI) right from the initial stages. Infrastructure can be represented with codes for easy deployment using tools such as CFEngine, Chef, Puppet, and PowerShell DSC. Microservices can be deployed using Docker or Kubernetes after containerization.

Testing microservices

We discussed the test pyramid representing the types of test. The unit test is used to verify small functionalities in the entire application, while a system test is used to verify the entire application on its functionality. The mock and stub approach is used in microservices testing. This approach makes testing independent of other microservices and eliminates challenges in testing the application's database due to mock database interactions. Integration testing is concerned with external microservices communicating with them in the process. This is done through mocking external services.

Security

Securing microservices is essential to an organization to ensure data integrity. In a monolithic application, security is attained by having a single point of authentication and authorization. However, this approach is not possible in microservices architecture, since each service needs to be secured independently. Therefore, the OAuth 2.0 authorization framework, coupled with OpenID Connect, is used to secure microservices. OAuth 2.0's main role is to authorize clients into the application system as we discussed in *chapter 7*. One provider of OAuth 2.0 and OpenID Connect is the Azure Active Directory (Azure AD)

Conclusive Remarks

It is our hope that this book has been essential in your understanding of the microservices architecture by answering all your questions based on this wide subject. Microservices architecture is a pretty new concept and is still in development. Therefore, the contents of this book may change over time.

Would appreciate if you could post a review on the purchasing platform!

Facebook: **@sflemingauthor**

Join the Author Page and group where I share the free codes of the audible releases!

ABOUT THE AUTHOR

Hello,

Welcome to my profile!

Here's my story:

I am Consultant (Project Management & Technology) in mid-thirties with a Bachelor in Engineering & Master in Business Management. I have worked in the areas of IT Advisory & Roadmap and Project Management for transformational projects. Currently, I am working for the public sector in e-Governance space and trying to take the benefits of technology to masses through innovation and customization. This aspect of disruptive technology beyond regular discussions/implementation excites me. I am always looking for that case study in South America, Africa or Asia where the rules of the game have been changed to serve the massive scale of the problem!

On the personal front, last 10 years have been a roller coaster ride managing career and family. Now my son has started going to school and daily routine is balanced and in control. So, I decided to launch my upgraded version! (I.e. I realigned my goals in the areas of Mindset, Career and passive income streams).

Other than Technology, I have been always inquisitive about the humane factors leading to success/failure. I always enjoyed the role of a career advisor, motivator in my organization and university. Autobiographies always attracted me and I have gone through many of them since my early days.

I have been working consistently and most importantly enjoying my current phase of life and growth. With all the experience and renewed vigor, I am sure to achieve my goals in stipulated time frame. I decided to jot down my learning and experiences along the way and share it with you.

Will See You Soon Friend!

Hello!

How was it?

If you liked the book kindly leave a review!

Any further suggestions: Kindly reach out at **valueadd2life@gmail.com**

Stephen Fleming (@sflemingauthor- Facebook Page)

Accelerated DevOps with AI, ML & RPA

Non-Programmer's Guide to AIOPS & MLOPS

ACCELERATED
DEVOPS
WITH
AI, ML & RPA

Non-Programmer's Guide
to AIOPS & MLOPS

STEPHEN FLEMING

INTRODUCTION

Technological advances such *as predictive analytics, auto computing (autonomics), artificial intelligence, and robotic process automation (RPA)* are currently motivating exceptional levels of automation in many other organizations. Put together; these three technological innovations are driving the next generation of automation-- what is regularly referred to as ***"intelligent or smart automation."*** Smart automation goes more than simple automation and orchestration of human tasks to integrate flexible self-learning-- leading to entirely autonomous systems. The Google car (and other similar solutions) is an excellent example of an intelligent automatic system capable of knowing from its environment and modifying attributes as necessary.

Automation in Classical DevOps

The electronic process is motivated through new-age modern technologies such as *social, mobile, big data, analytics, cloud, internet of things (IoT), artificial intelligence, augmented and virtual reality, genomics,* etc.

These solutions bring up considerable change and complexity to how modern systems are created and released. Enterprises that leverage these technologies to improve themselves into *intellectual enterprises* ask for fresh and smart methods. Such techniques and procedures need to be more than agile; they need to adaptive and capable of responding dynamically to frequently changing conditions.

Let's look at some samples of recent DevOps approaches and how they will need to evolve to support dynamic digital systems.

Automation within regular DevOps solutions is usually restricted to *scripting and orchestration*. Automation acceptance levels vary due to various reasons ranging from intricacy to skills and organizational challenges. Upkeep of such scripts is itself sometimes a bottleneck, as applications and environments change rapidly, new age agile, a digital company, by contrast, demand automation that is in a position to adapt dynamically and self-heal on the requirement.

Further, classic DevOps automation procedures are normally driven with predefined static rules. For example, the criteria for the promotion of an application build through various stages of the pipeline are often statically described. This is a restriction for new-age solutions where the *criteria need to be dynamic* and may vary based on multiple situations. The automation solution needs to able to look at past data, keep learning from recent data, and make flexible, intelligent forecasts about the right course of action.

DevOps for the (IoT) process is different than that for conventional software solutions. The intended environment for production deployment in consumer IoT is geographically scattered, typically not configuration managed, may have an undependable network connection, and may even be fragile. Further, IoT solutions generate huge amounts of data that demand robust data mining and self-learning (flexible) techniques not provided through traditional lifecycle automation tools.

Similarly, *customer experience (CX)* is a key new metric for online digital systems that transcends regular DevOps metrics, including release velocity and quality. CX data is disorganized, fuzzy, voluminous, and volatile. CX-driven DevOps (or CX-Ops) is an emerging discipline that requires big data analytics and intellectual strategies (including natural language processing or NLP) to decode meaningful insight from such data.

Hence, as digital enterprises develop and businesses demand greater agility and flexibility, the DevOps function to support such a process will need to change as well.

Intelligent DevOps: Era of Smart Automation Landscape

Right before we dive into what *intelligent DevOps* would look like, let's first look and feel at the several types of automatic systems being adapted in the marketplace in general. The following types of automation are defined as part of the "intelligent automation procession":

Solution that Does: These kinds of are standard automatic systems that replicate human keystroke actions and fixed (pre-defined) rules-based activities. They also take benefit of descriptive analytics that shows past fads and trends. Instances of such systems consist of speech and image recognition.

Solution that Think: These use formulas and knowledge to find the definition in data, manage judgment-oriented tasks using diagnostic analytics, and make referrals based on trends. Examples of such systems consist of natural language processing and recommendation engines (such as email spam filters).

Solution that Learn: These kinds of understand the context, translate and dynamically adjust based on scenarios; they normally take advantage of predictive and prescriptive analytics to solve problems separately. Examples of such systems include self-driving vehicles and neural networks.

A Peek at Intelligent DevOps

So, what would transformed smart DevOps look like? Smart DevOps automatic would take benefit of *cognitive and autonomics systems* to enable smarter adaptive lifecycle automatic based on analytics. Smart DevOps, to a substantial degree, relies on this kind of capability.

Based on the above model, let's check the variety of DevOps automatic we can work upon:

DevOps Solutions that Do: This includes *traditional DevOps automated systems* (e.g., for constant integration and testing, continuous deployment), as well as pipeline lifecycle automated that are based on static rules (e.g., traditional release management automatic).

DevOps Solutions that Think: This consists of advanced automation systems such as:

- Automated automation systems, for instance, generation of automated test cases from manual tests (or test models) using NLP, generation of virtual services based on request-response information logs.

- Self-healing automatic, for instance, virtual services (or test scripts) that can auto-update based on a change in application endpoints (or behavior).

- Surveillance of IoT systems, for example, *"smart homes,"* which require continuous use of diagnostic analytics to mine massive quantities of data to understand failing modes and recommend recovery techniques.

- Automated verification of system demands based on customer experience analytics.

- Self-production of test scenarios based on analytics on development logs.

DevOps Systems that Learn: This consists of sophisticated test automation systems such as:

- Flexible continuous delivery pipeline-- Discovering systems that analyze past data to manage the pipeline based on dynamic rules. For example, associate code top quality and flaw detection and slippage patterns to dynamically determine that which tests are to be run and which gates are to be enforced for various teams and products for promoting application builds

- DevOps procedure optimization based on insight throughout the life cycle. For example, the relationships of production log data with past code change data to determine the level of failure risk in different application components.

Cross-Life Cycle DevOps Intellect

Smart DevOps enables us to perform procedure optimization based on analytics from data correlated across the system life cycle, from planning through an operation. Each procedure area generates a great amount of data that is normally evaluated within the process (and sometimes organizational) silo.

While such analytics is useful in itself, the connection of data throughout these procedure areas may be used to provide a wide variety of intelligent lifecycle insight (and procedure improvement possibilities), such as:

- Correlating configuration data analytics with code change and flaw analytics helps us proactively recognize failing modes related to code and infrastructure changes.
- CX analytics (from the Operations procedure) can be used to validate requirements in the plan and define procedures
- Production log analytics may be associated to test log data to identify missing out on test cases. As per the "Continuous Delivery" concept in DevOps, we visualize a new option stream around "Continuous Insight" where analytical understandings are generated and acted upon continuously (and autonomously) as procedures carry out.

So, we believe that intelligent approaches described above will be infused into every aspect of DevOps going onward and reinvent the way DevOps is performed.

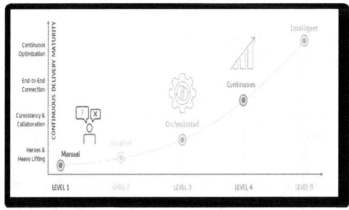

Diagram from Devops.com

The new DevOps with AI & ML

Modern technology advancements have taken the production abilities of firms to various limits practically across every market.

Long gone are the days where we use to see only human-intensive jobs!

Now, the world is high on technology-driven systems that eased industry processes, from developing a product to releasing it to the market and further towards offering a memorable experience to end-users.

DevOps is one technology service most heard in today's tech world, especially for boosted collaboration among teams and offering faster execution with less failure & high recovery rate.

In the IT industry, DevOps showed up as a solution for abilities such as continuous integration, continuous delivery, and accelerated development rate, among others, that can fasten the software process chain. That's not an end!

There are two of today's most advanced innovations that every other innovation or market would want to scale-up their performance and productivity. While some of the leading market players are already running on them, there are many medium and small-sized still on the run for them. They are undoubtedly **Artificial Intelligence (AI) and Machine Learning (ML)!**

Applying static tools for *deployments, provisioning, and Application Performance Monitoring (APM)* has currently seen its full potential and is getting soaked up by the ever-growing industry demands.

And, the next mission has already begun *for creative managing tools that can apply knowledge simplifying the task of development and testing engineers.* Here is where Ai and ML play vital roles!

We will see how AI and ML integrations can power DevOps. In brief, AI and ML help DevOps by automating routine & repeatable tasks; offering enhanced effectiveness, and minimizing teams' time spent on a procedure. Let's look into more details!

Basic Concepts: Cut the Clutter

__Artificial Intelligence__ is the wider principle of equipments being able to carry out jobs in a method that we would take into consideration "smart".

__Machine Learning__ is a current application of AI based around the idea that we need to actually simply be able to provide machines access to data as well as let them find out on their own.

AI in DevOps

A data revolution is one key aspect that is posing severe challenges to the DevOps atmosphere.

Checking through vast quantities of information to find an important issue as part of day-to-day computing operations is time-consuming and human-intensive.

That's where AI has its role in processing, evaluating, and making an instant decision that a human might take hours together to decide on.

With the evolution of DevOps, two different teams started collaborating on a single platform, which needs reliable tools that can reduce the event of errors and revisits a problem.

AI can transform the DevOps setting in various ways, such as:

- *Data Ease of access:* AI can increase the scope of data accessibility to the teams who typically face issues such as lack of freely-available data. AI improves the teams' ability to obtain accessibility to vast quantities of online data beyond business limits for big data gathering. It helps organizations to have well-organized information checked from widely-available datasets for *constant and repetitive evaluation.*

- *Self-governed Solutions:* Adjustment to change is one essential limiting that many firms have been facing owing to a lack of appropriate analytics that restrict themselves to certain borders. Whereas, AI has transformed the scenario bringing in a transition in analysis from being human to self-governed. Now, self-governed tools can drive many procedures that human beings might not be able to that quickly.

- *Resource Management:* Improving range for the production of automated atmospheres that run automate many routine and repeatable jobs, AI transformed the process of resource administration opening more methods for development and creating new techniques.

- *Software Development:* AI's capability to automate many of the service plans and support information analytics is common to have a more critical effect on DevOps atmosphere. Many firms have already begun taking on AI and Machine Learning for achieving effectiveness in application growth.

AI can help your groups in precisely determining the solution to your problem from a dataset rather than spending hours with each other on huge data volumes.

It not only saves time but also reduces the quantity of work.

Machine Learning (ML) impact on DevOps

ML System's too automated learning abilities speak the effective implementation of ML capabilities, which means making it culture the *'practice of continuous learning.'*

It is simpler for the team to deal with complex aspects such as linear styles, datasets, and query refining, and identifying new insights continuously at the speed of their executing platform.

Being part of the procedure chain, ML helps in easy repairing of code in case of bugs and streamlines the process.

Below areas defines the integration of ML and DevOps:

- *Application Progress:* While DevOps tools such as 'Git,' Ansible, among others provide the visibility of delivery procedure, applying ML to them addresses the irregularities around code quantities, long construct time, delays in code check-ins, slow launch rate, improper resourcing, and procedure slowdown, among others.

Hello!

How was it?

If you liked the promo, get it soon.

Any further suggestions: Kindly reach out at ***valueadd2life@gmail.com***

Stephen Fleming (@sflemingauthor- Facebook Page)